BATTLE OF THE MASK MAKERS

Story by Ryder Windham
Art by Caravan Studio

Little, Brown Books for Young Readers
www.lbkids.co.uk

LITTLE, BROWN BOOKS FOR YOUNG READERS

First published in the United States in 2016 by Little, Brown and Company
First published in Great Britain in 2016 by Hodder and Stoughton

1 3 5 7 9 10 8 6 4 2

LEGO, the LEGO logo, BIONICLE
and the BIONICLE logo are trademarks of the LEGO Group.

Produced by Hodder and Stoughton under license
from the LEGO Group. © 2016 The LEGO Group

Line art by Faisal P
Colors by Felix H, Angie, Kate, Indra, Depinz, Ifan, Amel, Sony, Surya

A CIP catalogue record for this book
is available from the British Library.

ISBN 978-1-51020-054-8

Printed in the United States of America

Little, Brown Books for Young Readers
An imprint of
Hachette Children's Group
Part of Hodder and Stoughton
Carmelite House
50 Victoria Embankment
London EC4Y 0DZ

An Hachette UK Company
www.hachette.co.uk

www.hachettechildrens.co.uk

THE PROPHECY

It was pieced together by fragments, whispered to the people of Okoto thousands of years ago when they found the motionless body of Ekimu the Mask Maker. The prophecy has been told around the campfire as part of the legacy of the Protectors, and handed down through the generations from father to son...

When times are dark
and all hope seems lost,

The Protectors
must unite,

One from each tribe,

Evoke the power of
past and future

And look to the skies
for an answer.

When the stars align,

Six comets will bring
timeless heroes

To claim the
masks of power

And find the Mask Maker.

United, the elements hold
the power to defeat evil.

United but not one.

TOA TAHU
MASTER OF
FIRE

Tahu is hot-tempered and brave. He likes to excel and thinks of himself as the most heroic of the heroes. His forgetful nature has gotten him into trouble at times, but Tahu seems to have been born under a very lucky star and somehow always comes out on top.

TOA KOPAKA
MASTER OF
ICE

Kopaka is noble and reserved. Upholding his own strict moral code, he strives to be perfect and always "do the right thing," a fact that often makes him appear formal and even cold in the eyes of others. Luckily, Kopaka's clumsiness and his not-too-solid sense of direction help the other heroes remember that, after all, Kopaka is just a Toa like them.

ONUA MASTER OF EARTH

Onua is grounded and wise. He likes to spend his time alone meditating under the stars. Like an underground cave, he is receptive and silent—except when he snores! Though Onua rarely says a word, the other heroes have come to respect this sleepy giant. They know that when he speaks, his crude voice carries guidance and wisdom.

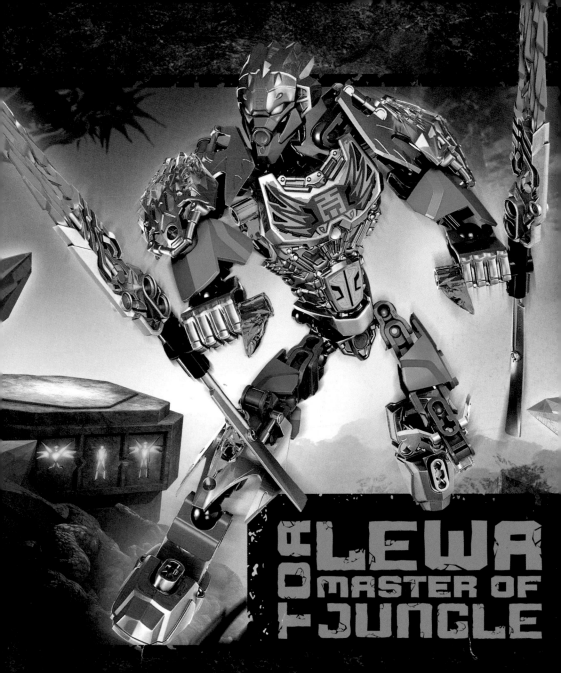

TOA LEWA
MASTER OF
JUNGLE

Lewa is a true daredevil, a fast-talking and witty adventurer whose foolhardy manners have often gotten him into trouble. His rebel approach is a double-edged sword that the other heroes both love and hate. On one hand, Lewa finds new ways of doing things; on the other, these ways sometimes lead to new trouble!

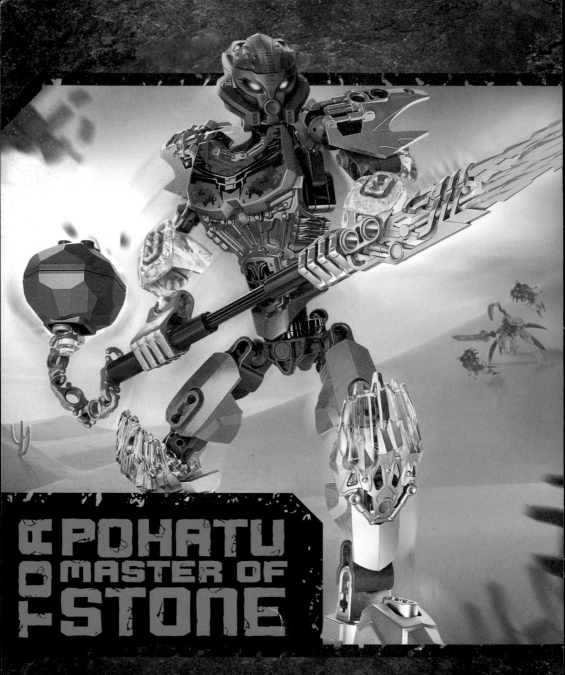

10 ✗ POHATU
MASTER OF
STONE

Pohatu is unyielding and fearless. Renowned for his unbreakable stamina, he is arguably the toughest of all the heroes. With firm resolution and mysterious stubbornness, Pohatu strides forward as a fearless vanguard leading the way for the heroes. Well, almost fearless. Pohatu does *not* like scorpions.

TOA GALI
MASTER OF WATER

Gali is friendly and peaceful. But when the situation calls for it, she can be as fierce as a raging ocean. She finds injustice intolerable and always goes out of her way to help the ones who need it. Gali's mellow ways have made her the most liked among the heroes. She is generous and a good listener and friend. Only one little thing: She just can't seem to tell a joke right!

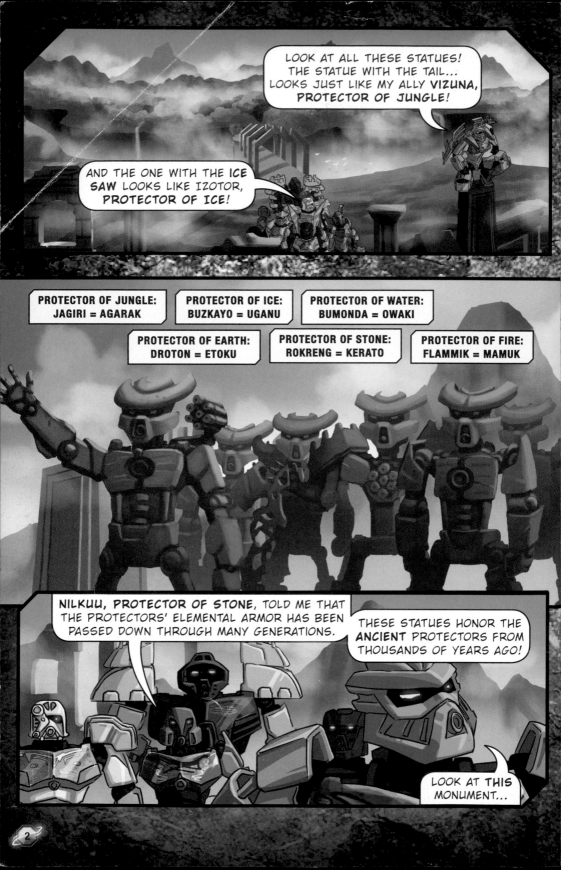

LOOK AT ALL THESE STATUES! THE STATUE WITH THE TAIL... LOOKS JUST LIKE MY ALLY **VIZUNA**, **PROTECTOR OF JUNGLE!**

AND THE ONE WITH THE **ICE SAW** LOOKS LIKE IZOTOR, **PROTECTOR OF ICE!**

PROTECTOR OF JUNGLE: JAGIRI = AGARAK	PROTECTOR OF ICE: BUZKAYO = UGANU	PROTECTOR OF WATER: BUMONDA = OWAKI
PROTECTOR OF EARTH: DROTON = ETOKU	PROTECTOR OF STONE: ROKRENG = KERATO	PROTECTOR OF FIRE: FLAMMIK = MAMUK

NILKUU, **PROTECTOR OF STONE**, TOLD ME THAT THE PROTECTORS' ELEMENTAL ARMOR HAS BEEN PASSED DOWN THROUGH MANY GENERATIONS.

THESE STATUES HONOR THE **ANCIENT** PROTECTORS FROM THOUSANDS OF YEARS AGO!

LOOK AT **THIS** MONUMENT...

2

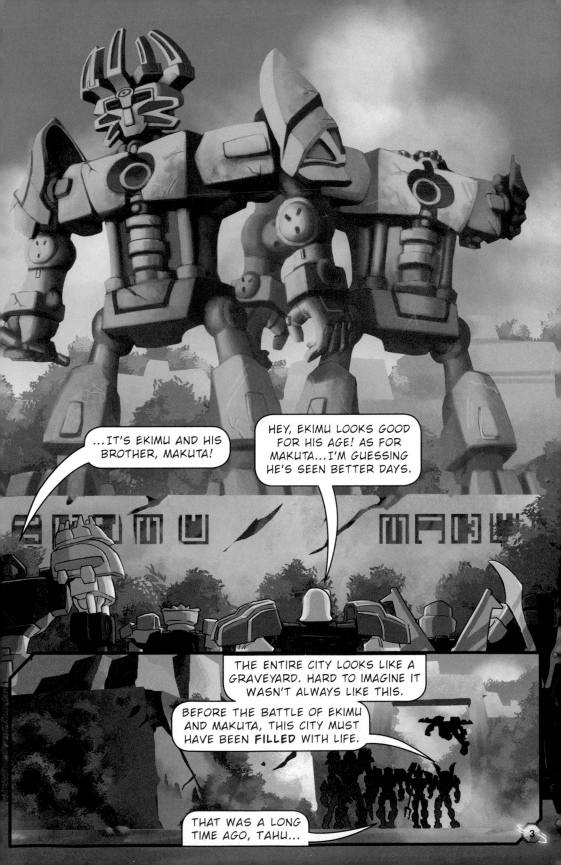

FOR MANY GENERATIONS, THE PROTECTORS AND THEIR DESCENDANTS HAVE SERVED AS GUARDIANS OF THE SIX ELEMENTAL REGIONS OF OKOTO.

THEY HELP US IN TIMES OF NEED, DURING EMERGENCIES AND NATURAL DISASTERS, AND IN DEFENSE AGAINST WILD BEASTS!

TODAY, AT OUR FESTIVAL OF MASKS, WE GATHER TO HONOR THE PROTECTORS FOR THEIR COURAGE AND ONGOING SERVICE, AND FOR HELPING US STAY UNITED!

MAKUTA, WOULD YOU LIKE TO SAY ANYTHING?

...I HOPE TO PAY THEM BACK.

JUST A FEW WORDS.

PLEASE JOIN ME IN THANKING THE PROTECTORS FOR THEIR SERVICE. WE OWE THEM SO MUCH, AND SOMEDAY...

THE FESTIVAL WON'T LAST FOREVER. ENJOY IT WHILE YOU CAN!

LONG LIVE THE MASK MAKERS AND THE PROTECTORS!

HOORAY!

HOORAY!

7

WELCOME TO THE **FORGE!** PLEASE FORGIVE THE CLUTTER...

...BUT IT APPEARS MAKUTA HAS BEEN BUSY AND NEGLECTED TO TIDY UP.

NO NEED TO APOLOGIZE, EKIMU. YOUR WORKSHOP IS A **WONDROUS** PLACE, AND WE ARE HONORED TO VISIT.

AH! **THIS** IS WHERE THE **MAGIC** HAPPENS...!

...THE **ANVILS** OF THE **MASK MAKERS!**

EKIMU, ANY IDEA OF HOW MANY MASKS YOU'VE CRAFTED OVER THE YEARS?

MORE THAN I CAN REMEMBER. BUT ALLOW ME TO SHOW YOU MY MOST RECENT WORK!

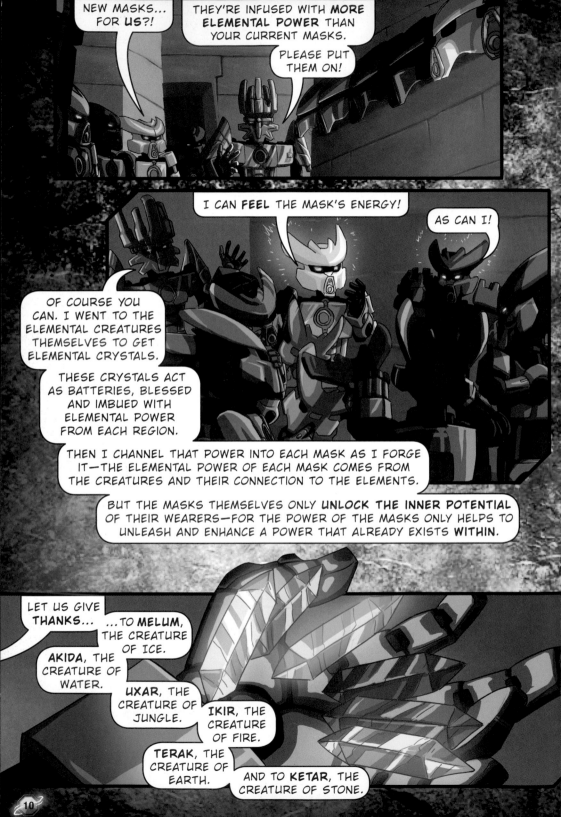

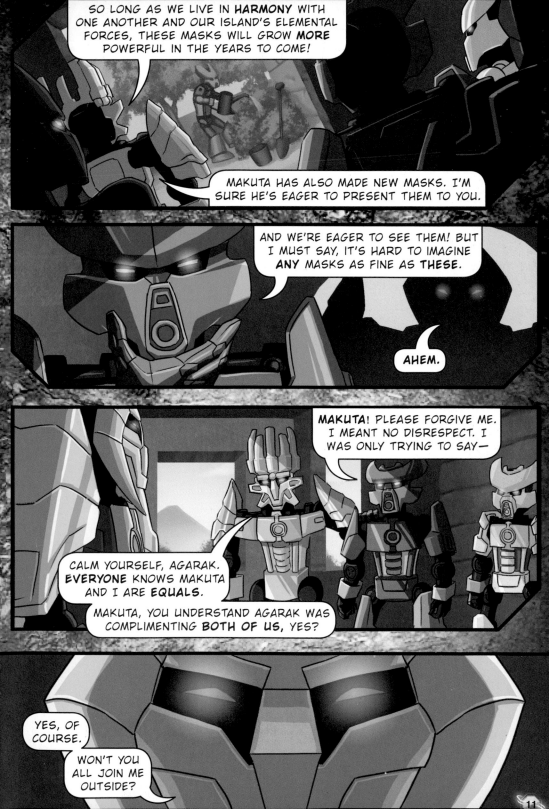

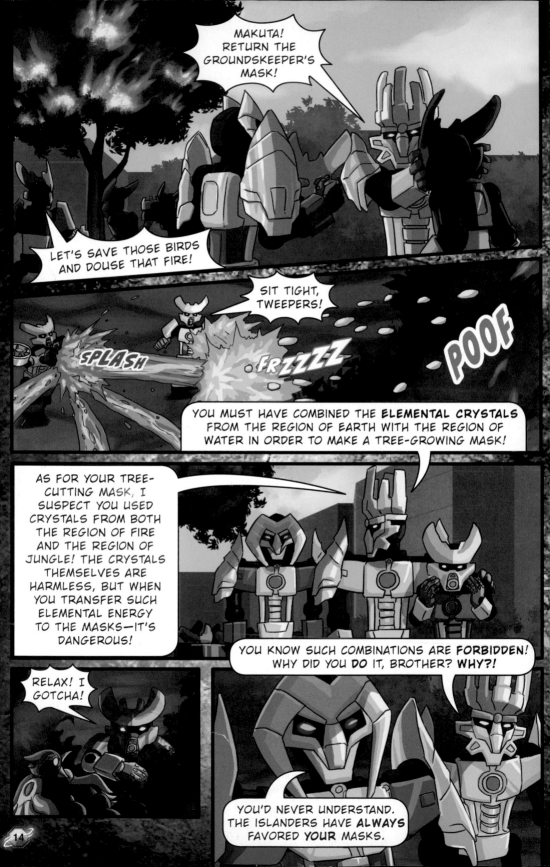

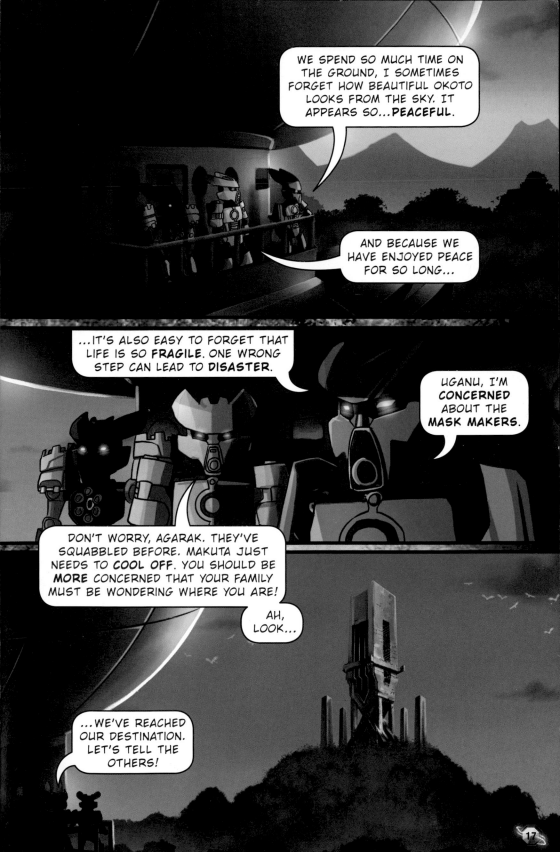

WE SPEND SO MUCH TIME ON THE GROUND, I SOMETIMES FORGET HOW BEAUTIFUL OKOTO LOOKS FROM THE SKY. IT APPEARS SO...**PEACEFUL.**

AND BECAUSE WE HAVE ENJOYED PEACE FOR SO LONG...

...IT'S ALSO EASY TO FORGET THAT LIFE IS SO **FRAGILE.** ONE WRONG STEP CAN LEAD TO **DISASTER.**

UGANU, I'M **CONCERNED** ABOUT THE **MASK MAKERS.**

DON'T WORRY, AGARAK. THEY'VE SQUABBLED BEFORE. MAKUTA JUST NEEDS TO **COOL OFF.** YOU SHOULD BE **MORE** CONCERNED THAT YOUR FAMILY MUST BE WONDERING WHERE YOU ARE!

AH, LOOK...

...WE'VE REACHED OUR DESTINATION. LET'S TELL THE OTHERS!

ACCORDING TO HISTORIANS, THE **TEMPLE OF TIME** IS THE OLDEST STRUCTURE ON OKOTO, BUT THE **MASK OF TIME** IS EVEN **OLDER!**

OLDER THAN OUR ANCESTORS WHO NAMED THE **SIX REGIONS OF OKOTO** AFTER THE **ELEMENTAL CREATURES.**

OLDER THAN OKOTO ITSELF. OLDER THAN OUR WORLD. OLDER THAN THE **STARS!**

LEGEND HAS IT THAT THE ANCIENT NAME FOR THE MASK OF TIME WAS **VAHI**, AND THAT IT ONCE CONSISTED OF TWO PIECES. **THIS** PIECE IS THE UPPER HALF.

THE MASK CAN GIVE VIEWS INTO THE PAST AND FUTURE, AND INTO FARAWAY REALMS BEYOND OUR IMAGININGS.

WHEN IT SHOWS THE FUTURE, DOES IT REVEAL WHAT **MAY** HAPPEN OR WHAT **WILL** HAPPEN?

TOA?

EKIMU? CAN YOU HEAR ME?

GET THAT MASK OFF HIM AND PUT HIS OWN MASK BACK ON!

CAREFUL!

EKIMU! ARE YOU ALL RIGHT?

YOU SAID SOMETHING THAT SOUNDED LIKE "TOH-UH," AND THEN YOU COLLAPSED!

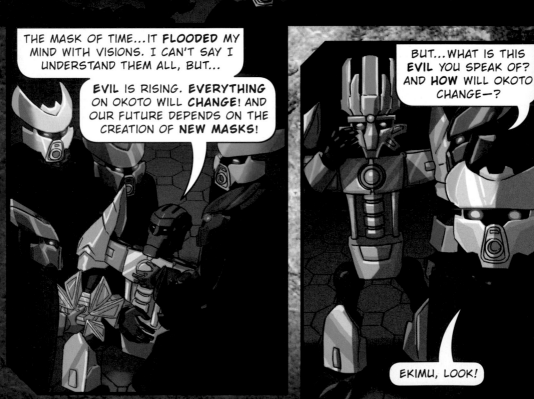

THE MASK OF TIME...IT FLOODED MY MIND WITH VISIONS. I CAN'T SAY I UNDERSTAND THEM ALL, BUT...

EVIL IS RISING. EVERYTHING ON OKOTO WILL CHANGE! AND OUR FUTURE DEPENDS ON THE CREATION OF NEW MASKS!

BUT...WHAT IS THIS EVIL YOU SPEAK OF? AND HOW WILL OKOTO CHANGE—?

EKIMU, LOOK!

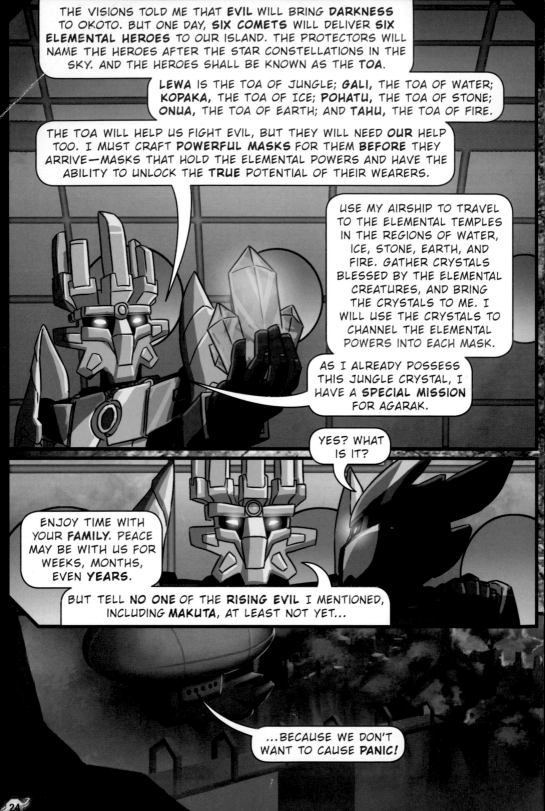

THE VISIONS TOLD ME THAT **EVIL** WILL BRING **DARKNESS** TO OKOTO. BUT ONE DAY, **SIX COMETS** WILL DELIVER **SIX ELEMENTAL HEROES** TO OUR ISLAND. THE PROTECTORS WILL NAME THE HEROES AFTER THE STAR CONSTELLATIONS IN THE SKY. AND THE HEROES SHALL BE KNOWN AS THE **TOA.**

LEWA IS THE TOA OF JUNGLE; **GALI,** THE TOA OF WATER; **KOPAKA,** THE TOA OF ICE; **POHATU,** THE TOA OF STONE; **ONUA,** THE TOA OF EARTH; AND **TAHU,** THE TOA OF FIRE.

THE TOA WILL HELP US FIGHT EVIL, BUT THEY WILL NEED **OUR** HELP TOO. I MUST CRAFT **POWERFUL MASKS** FOR THEM **BEFORE** THEY ARRIVE—MASKS THAT HOLD THE ELEMENTAL POWERS AND HAVE THE ABILITY TO UNLOCK THE **TRUE** POTENTIAL OF THEIR WEARERS.

USE MY AIRSHIP TO TRAVEL TO THE ELEMENTAL TEMPLES IN THE REGIONS OF WATER, ICE, STONE, EARTH, AND FIRE. GATHER CRYSTALS BLESSED BY THE ELEMENTAL CREATURES, AND BRING THE CRYSTALS TO ME. I WILL USE THE CRYSTALS TO CHANNEL THE ELEMENTAL POWERS INTO EACH MASK.

AS I ALREADY POSSESS THIS JUNGLE CRYSTAL, I HAVE A **SPECIAL MISSION** FOR AGARAK.

YES? WHAT IS IT?

ENJOY TIME WITH YOUR **FAMILY.** PEACE MAY BE WITH US FOR WEEKS, MONTHS, EVEN **YEARS.**

BUT TELL **NO ONE** OF THE **RISING EVIL** I MENTIONED, INCLUDING **MAKUTA,** AT LEAST NOT YET...

...BECAUSE WE DON'T WANT TO CAUSE **PANIC!**

MASTER MAKUTA! MASTER MAKUTA!

WHAT IS IT?

YOU ASKED ME TO WATCH FOR MASTER EKIMU'S AIRSHIP. IT'S APPROACHING **NOW!**

I BELIEVE THE PROTECTORS ARE WITH HIM. SHALL WE GO GREET THEM?

YES, MASTER MAKUTA.

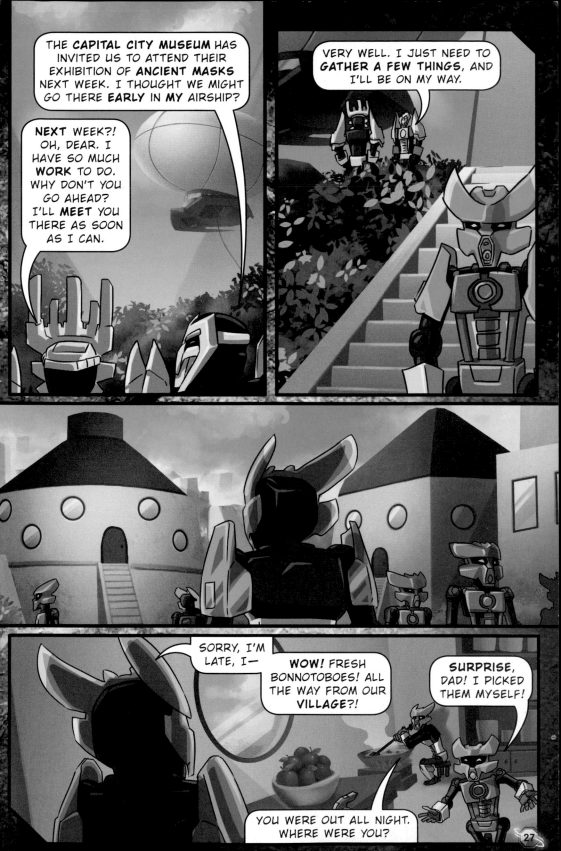

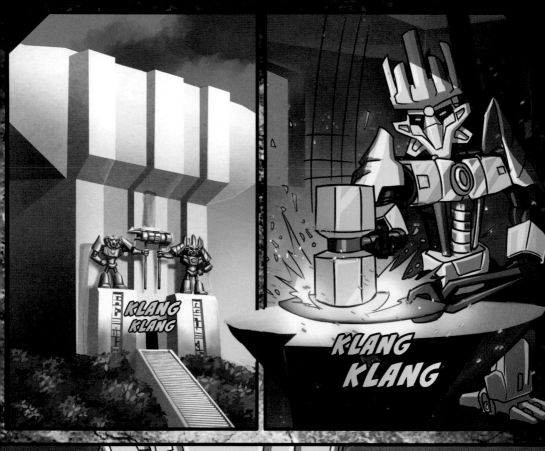

THANK YOU, IKIR!

HURRY, KERATO! WE CAN'T KEEP EKIMU WAITING!

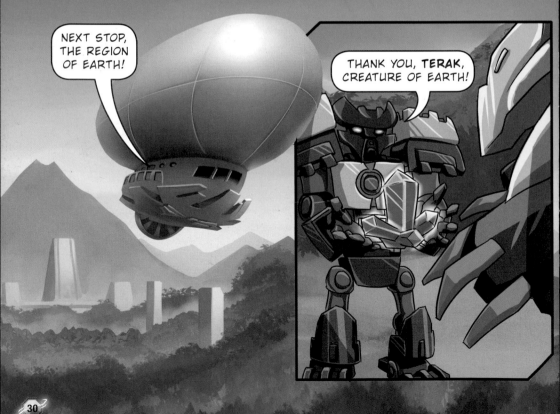

NEXT STOP, THE REGION OF EARTH!

THANK YOU, **TERAK**, CREATURE OF EARTH!

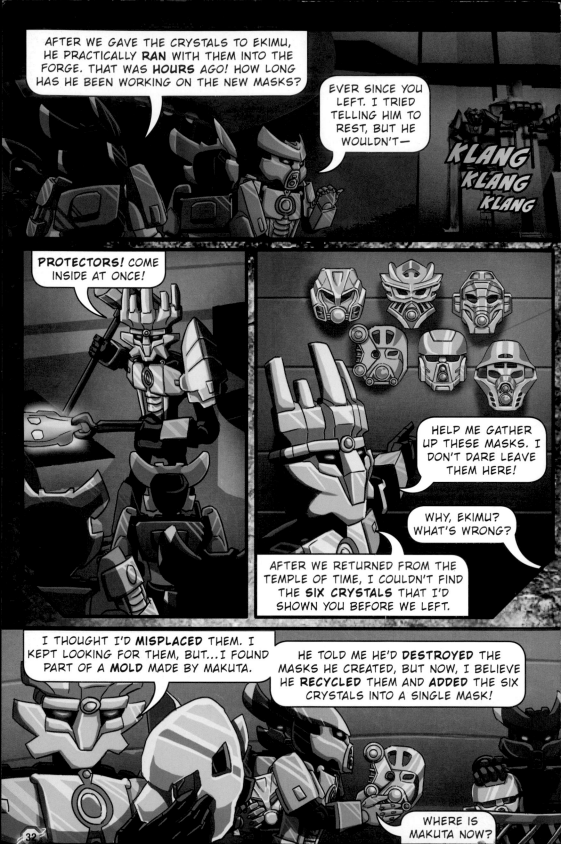

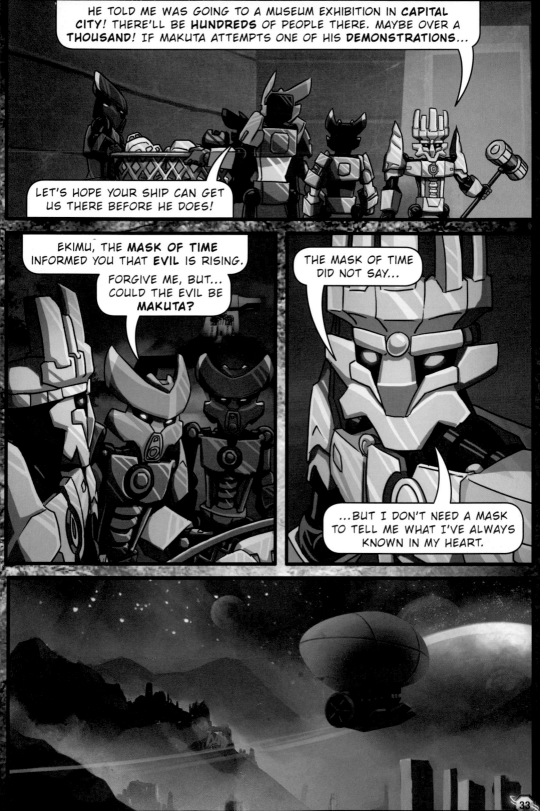

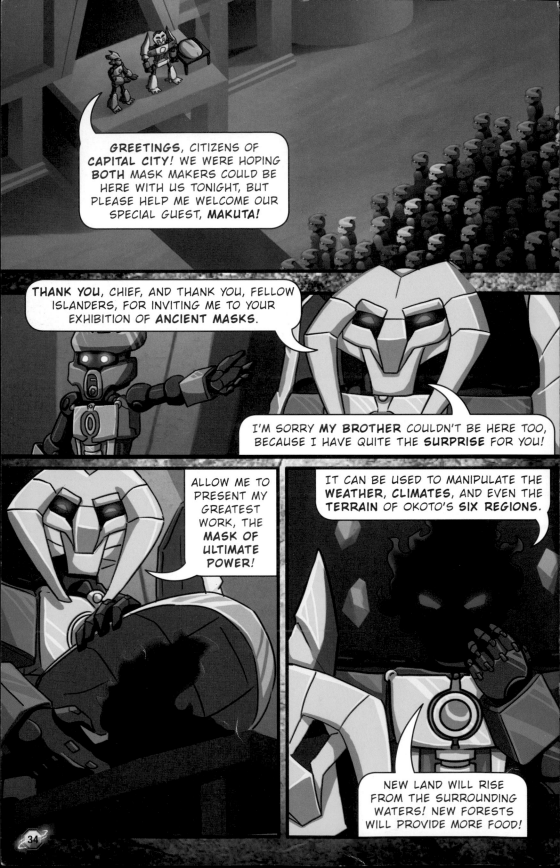

THE OTHER PROTECTORS...?

WE ALL SURVIVED. BUT CAPITAL CITY... IT'S **GONE**, AGARAK.

ALL THE TOA MASKS ARE LOST TOO.

IS...IS SOMEONE WHISPERING? I HEAR—

I HEAR IT TOO.

WE **ALL** DO. IT'S COMING FROM OVER THERE!

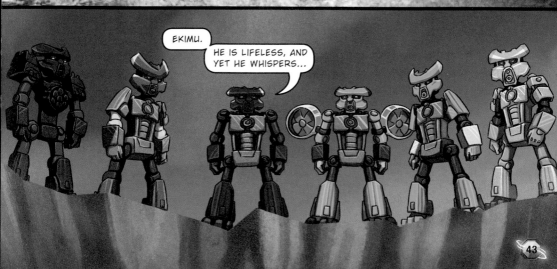

EKIMU. HE IS LIFELESS, AND YET HE WHISPERS...

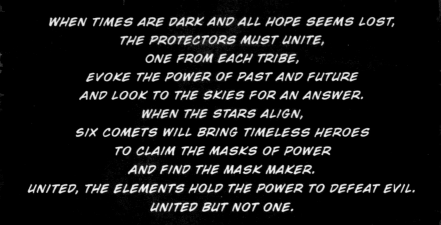

WHEN TIMES ARE DARK AND ALL HOPE SEEMS LOST,
THE PROTECTORS MUST UNITE,
ONE FROM EACH TRIBE,
EVOKE THE POWER OF PAST AND FUTURE
AND LOOK TO THE SKIES FOR AN ANSWER.
WHEN THE STARS ALIGN,
SIX COMETS WILL BRING TIMELESS HEROES
TO CLAIM THE MASKS OF POWER
AND FIND THE MASK MAKER.
UNITED, THE ELEMENTS HOLD THE POWER TO DEFEAT EVIL.
UNITED BUT NOT ONE.

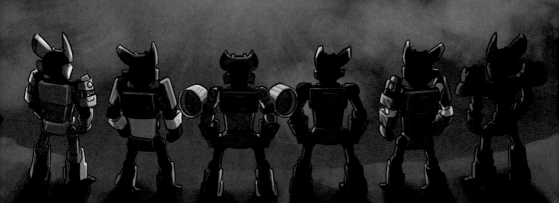

IT'S A **PROPHECY**...AND THE TIMELESS HEROES MUST BE THE **TOA!**

I...I MUST FIND OUT IF MY FAMILY SURVIVED THE BLAST.

THEN LET US GO WITH YOU, AND WE'LL RETURN EKIMU'S BODY TO THE CITY OF THE MASK MAKERS. WE'D BEST GET GOING. WITHOUT AN AIRSHIP, THE JOURNEY WILL TAKE MANY DAYS.

TO **FIND** ALL THE MASKS OF POWER EKIMU CREATED FOR THE TOA, IT MAY TAKE **YEARS**...OR **CENTURIES!**

THEN IF **WE** DON'T FIND THE MASKS, THE **DUTY** WILL FALL TO OUR **HEIRS!**

THE DAMAGE DOESN'T LOOK SO BAD FROM HERE.

THE CITY MUST HAVE BEEN PROTECTED FROM THE BLAST BY THE MOUNTAINS...

TWEEP TWEEP TWEEP

I TOLD YOU DAD WOULD COME BACK, MOM! I TOLD YOU!

WHERE WERE YOU? WHAT HAPPENED?

I'LL TELL YOU EVERYTHING. BUT LATER...**AFTER** WE LAY EKIMU TO REST.

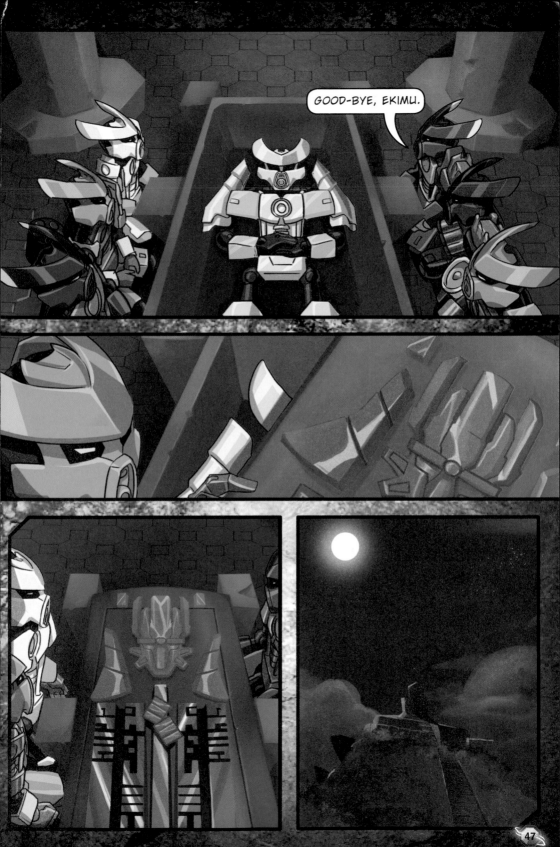

THE OKOTO PROTECTORS GUIDE

THE PROTECTORS GUIDE

After the Toa revive Ekimu the Mask Maker, they work with the Protectors to restore the City of the Mask Makers to its former glory. While rebuilding the city, the Protectors examine various ancient artifacts that illustrate their ancestors' history on the island and the events that led to the battle between Ekimu and his evil brother, Makuta. By studying the past, the Protectors hope to help their fellow islanders and find new ways to fight the dangerous monsters that threaten Okoto.

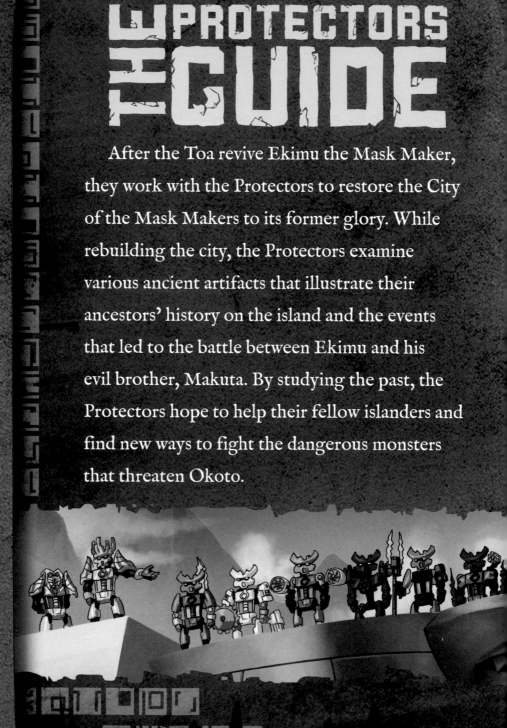

MAP OF OKOTO

Before the Battle of the Mask Makers radically transformed Okoto's geographic features, the island was almost completely covered by jungle forests. However, ancient islanders were aware that Okoto possessed six distinct elemental energies, and that each of these energies was especially strong  in specific areas. These areas became known as the six regions, and each region is home to six respective immortal elemental creatures.

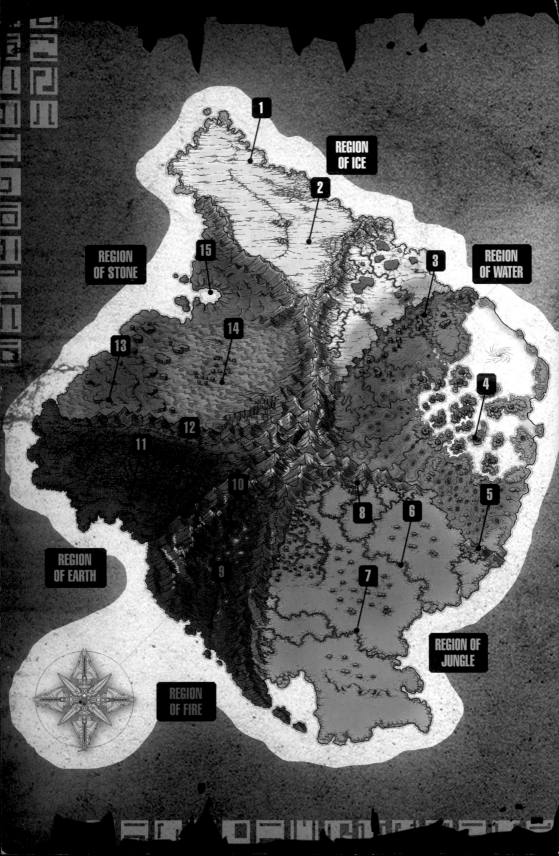

Lost Cities

Totally destroyed during the Battle of the Mask Makers, the area once occupied by Capital City is now known as the Great Crater. The powerful blast destroyed other cities across the island.

Surviving Structures

Okoto's mountain ranges shielded the Temple of Time, many buildings in the City of the Mask Makers, and other

areas of the Region of Jungle from the devastating shock wave that altered the island's surface.

ELEMENTAL CREATURES

According to ancient lore, the six elemental creatures of Okoto may be as old as the island itself. Each creature represents one of the six primal elemental forces of the island. Ancient islanders built temples to honor the creatures, who continue to reside within the temples. Despite their incredible age and power, the creatures were unable to prevent the cataclysm that reshaped Okoto.

Creature of Ice

Name: Melum

Powers: Controls the element of ice, possesses great strength, and attacks with sharp ice-crystal claws

Creature of Water

Name: Akida

Powers: Controls the element of water and can swim at hyper speeds

Creature of Jungle

Name: Uxar

Powers: Controls the plants and jungles of Okoto and can fly at supersonic speeds

Creature of Fire

Name: Ikir

Powers: Controls the element of fire and flies on wings of fire

Creature of Earth

Name: Terak

Powers: Controls the element of earth, possesses incredible strength, and travels through the ground with remarkable speed

Creature of Stone

Name: Ketar

Powers: Controls the element of stonefire, uses powerful claws for digging and fighting, and is equipped with a stinger to stun enemies

ANCIENT PROTECTORS

During the reign of the Mask Makers, the ancient Protectors who served Okoto wore elemental masks and armor that they inherited from their forefathers. Although the Protectors and their descendants must occasionally modify and repair their armor and weapons, their outward physical appearances have remained essentially unchanged for thousands of years.

Protector of Ice

Name: Uganu

Weapons: Elemental ice blaster, ice saw

Protector of Water

Name: Owaki

Weapons: Elemental torpedo blaster, two propulsion turbines

Protector of Jungle

Name: Agarak

Weapons: Air elemental flame bow, sensor tail

Protector of Fire

Name: Mamuk

Weapons: Elemental fire blaster, two flame swords

Protector of Earth

Name: Etoku

Weapons: Rapid shooter, two throwing knives, adamantine star drill

Protector of Stone

Name: Kerato

Weapon: Elemental sandstone blaster

CITY OF THE MASK MAKERS

In ancient times, many islanders lived in the City of the Mask Makers, which was named after Okoto's most celebrated craftsmen, the brothers Ekimu and Makuta. Because masks have always been an extremely important part of Okoto culture, the contributions of Ekimu and Makuta transformed the city into a center of arts and industry.

Although much of the city remained intact after the cataclysm, the surviving population sensed the presence of a rising evil, and they fled to smaller villages elsewhere. Over time, the evil grew stronger, attracting monsters that claimed the city as their own.

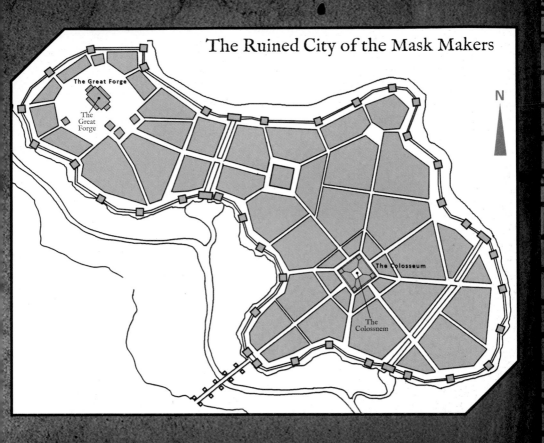

The Ruined City of the Mask Makers

The Great Forge

The
Great
Forge

N

The Colosseum

The
Colossuem

After Ekimu's revival, the Toa and the Protectors defeated most of the monsters and drove them out of the city. Since then, the heroes have begun to rebuild the city and have invited islanders to help restore and colonize the long-abandoned buildings.

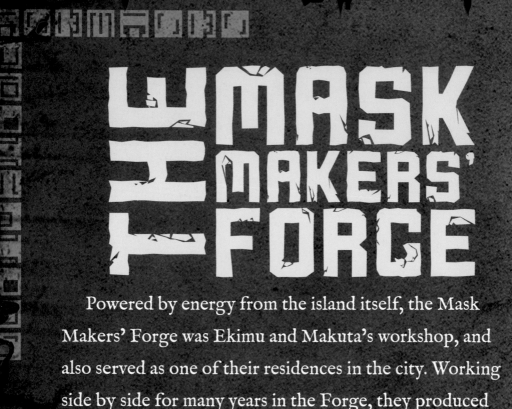

THE MASK MAKERS' FORGE

Powered by energy from the island itself, the Mask Makers' Forge was Ekimu and Makuta's workshop, and also served as one of their residences in the city. Working side by side for many years in the Forge, they produced masks for many islanders, including the Protectors.

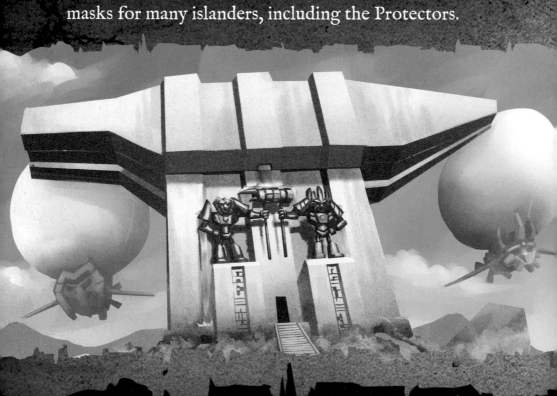

Ekimu anticipated that a great evil would gain power over Okoto and that the Protectors would need to summon six mighty heroes from beyond time and space to fight that evil. Using energy crystals from across the island, Ekimu created powerful masks for the heroes, but during his climactic battle with Makuta, the masks became scattered across the island. The Protectors sealed off the Forge, and it lay dormant for centuries. Ekimu has since reclaimed his Forge and resumed the production of masks.

EKIMU'S HAMMER

The Sacred Hammer of Power was Ekimu's primary tool and weapon. Ekimu used this hammer to craft Masks of Power for the Toa before he used it in battle against Makuta.

THE MASK MAKERS' AIRSHIPS

During their long reign on Okoto, Ekimu and Makuta used their own airships to travel across Okoto. These fantastic vehicles were made of lightweight metals and enabled the brothers to fly over mountains and go from one end of the island to another within a single day. They routinely flew their airships on missions to each of the six regions, where they would gather crystals for use in the

production of masks. During national emergencies, they allowed the Protectors to borrow the airships.

Both airships were destroyed during the Battle of the Mask Makers. Because the cataclysm shattered the island's natural energy fields, the Protectors doubt such vessels can ever fly again. The revived Ekimu still possesses the plans for his airship and is confident he can build a new one.

FESTIVAL OF MASKS

There was a time when islanders from all over Okoto would gather in the City of the Mask Makers for the annual Festival of Masks. The festival was an occasion to celebrate Okoto's heroes and to honor the age-old tradition of wearing masks, which helped keep the tribes united.

Islanders have not celebrated the Festival of Masks since before the Battle of the Mask Makers. Shortly after awakening from his long sleep, Ekimu, with the Protectors, begins organizing a new Festival of Masks!

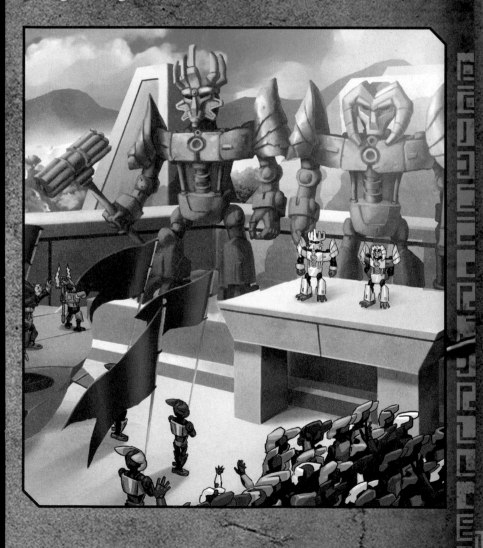